I0165269

"My Love Letters To God"

Anita M. Davis

ISBN: 0692739602
ISBN-13: 978-0692739600

DEDICATION

I give honor to my parents Robert L Davis, Sr. and Beverly J. Nelson for creating and birthing me with my very life. Without you there would be no me! I love you both and thanks for all that you do. I'm so grateful for your love and support!

I am a strong woman today because of your strong upbringing, of good morals and values. You taught me to be a leader and not a follower, and to go after what I want in life. With that being said; I am now doing one of my greatest passions, which is writing my Christian Poetry to share with the world by encouraging and uplifting others.

I'm doing what I love to do so it's not "work" because I enjoy writing poetry. I'm all grown up now and doing what I like to do and how I like to do it "my way."

Thank you so much for allowing me to be me, I hope you both are proud of me because I know God is!

DEDICATION

This poetry book began and was birthed because my late Great-Grandmother (Lillian Frieson) God rest her soul, instructed me to write and journal my day to day thoughts to God. She told me that she may not always be here and God would always be, so I should tell God all about things I would face in life.

In school at the age of ten I began my love letters to God even though I didn't even realize it. I was inspired through the words of my Gramma to tell God my hearts cry and desires. He listened and He became my best friend when Gramma couldn't be at elementary school with me.

I would cry when my feelings were hurt by the other children at school as they bullied me because of jealousy and just plain meanness. I learned to go to a quiet place at school, which was in the bathroom or in a corner of the playground and I would talk to God about what was going on.

I began to notice after praying to God I would feel better and I was able to smile again. Just as Gramma hoped and instructed me to do in her absence. This started the healing journey through me writing words that became my written prayers.

Thank you Gramma for instilling in me that God is strong, powerful, loving and He can handle my bullies and restore my heart and mind to a better place.

God became my soft place to fall in hard times. Those hard times became better for the good times ahead.

He always made me feel better so I wouldn't always be bitter!

This book is dedicated to my Great-Gramma who gave me the foundation to bring "My Love Letters To God" to life.

<u>My Faith in Him</u>

God has never forsaken me. My love and trust in Him never
wavered, no matter what my physical eyes would see; or what my
heart was feeling at the time.

Because I was taught that I am His child and he would be attentive to
my cry for help. I have always believed God would hear my prayers
and he would respond to me.

CONTENTS
First Segment

ACKNOWLEDGMENTS

I would like to first acknowledge and thank my Lord and Savior Jesus Christ for saving me, and giving me the gift of writing.

To all my siblings biological, step, God brothers and sisters; I thank you for all your love and support over the years. You're the best brothers and sisters a girl could have. Thank you for always being there for me, because that is what we do.

To my Pastors Joseph Walker and Co-Pastor Lady Kim Walker; thanks for loving on me, teaching, supporting and allowing me to go forth in my poetry ministry at RCF (Restoration Christian Fellowship Church). You both are so important and inspirational to me in my gift of writing. I truly love and appreciate you both for your covering and instructions. May God continue to bless you real good...

To Bishop Joey Johnson and Co-Pastor Lady Cathy Johnson from "The House of the Lord Church" in Akron Ohio; thanks for accepting me into your hearts, and family. I have always been so appreciative from the first moment I got saved in 1987 and joined THOTL when my little sister Crystal Denise Davis gave me direction by encouraging me and brought me to her church. I proudly joined and served in several ministries for many years under the leadership of Bishop. Thank you for loving me, and teaching me that, I am worthy of love.

Your parents Evelyn and Flanvis Johnson whom I affectionately called "Mommy and Elder" thank you for taking me under your wing as my spiritual mother and father. Even though you're both gone now, but you will never ever be forgotten. My heart has so many loving memories of you! All your unconditional love does my heart good even to this day.

Franky, you are such an encouraging brother to me. Thanks for speaking into my life and seeing my poetry ministry. I remember the prophetic word that you saw. "Five books being birthed out of me." Praise God! Here is the first one.

My God Mothers: Mrs. Laura Stewart, Mrs. Mattie Smith, Mrs. Ilean Willingham, for your unconditional love over the years. Your love and support has been unwavering and limitless. To God be the Glory for Mothers always loving on me speaking into me, and praying for me. I'm so blessed to have you in my life!

To my personal and dear friends, too many to name; you know who you are! Your continual love is the glue that holds me together on a daily basis. I am so blessed to have such and awesome group of men and women who love on me, and pray for me as you all do. Don't ever stop because I really need that strong and loving friendship that keeps me feeling loved and encouraged.

To all my other relatives; your love and support means so much. I know that you all are proud of me and please continue to pray my strength.

To all the Nay-sayers who have been negative and hurt me over the years for one reason or another; and thought I would crumble. All I can say is, "But God...!" God's unconditional Love is all that I need in my life. What God has for me is for me! There is a saying, "What doesn't kill you will make you stronger!" God's strength is made perfect in my weakness... God is able to see me through all things!

<u>Words From My Heart</u>

I'm alive and still here! Praise God I'm still standing in Jesus name! After I have done all I can, I just stand... To God be the Glory for the things He has done; and not yet done! For Christ I live and for Christ I die... Thank You Jesus for believing that I am worthy of your love and gifts!

You said, my gifts would make room for me! Yes Lord, You just knew! Praise God for knowing me even in my mother's womb...
I'm so glad I was able to make you smile and that I'm the apple of your eye.

This is the day that the Lord hath made, I will rejoice and be glad in it.

Thank you Jesus we did it!!!

All Biblical paraphrases or quotes in this poetry book that relates, or in similarity to the word of God; are used intentionally. They have been purposely taken from the greatest book in the world known as the Bible (KJV/NIV).

"My Love Letters To God"

Anita M. Davis

God's Dunamis Power

God's Dunamis power still works
It is strong, powerful, and mighty

It's the gift that keeps going when we are tired,
Weak and ready to give up

God's Dunamis power gives me the continued strength
To make it yet another day

When I'm feeling lonely and depressed
God smiles on me and tells me
I can make it because He will fight
My battles for me

There is no greater power…

There is no greater love…

God just shows up and shows out in all our circumstances
With His Dunamis power

His Dunamis power heals us
It strengthens us
It protects and provides

But God; only God
Praise God from whom all our blessings flow

Thank God because He just is all Dunamis
All by Himself…

I Know the Blood Still Works

I know the blood still works
Because I am nothing without Him
He lets me know that I am His own

I was bought with a price

His blood shed saved me, changed me,
Made me a new creature in Him

His blood still works because I'm not what I use to be
I'm better, a little better every day because of Him

He is perfect in my weakness
Because he thought I was worth saving

I won't give up on God because He won't give up on me
He's able to see me through all things!

My God's power still works…
His blood shed still works…
His love for me still works…

Beauty for Ashes

God wants to look good on you
Receive His Glory today

He wants to turn your life around
He wants to make you brand new

Bring you into a transformation
Of goodness and healing

Turning your mourning into dancing
Beauty for ashes

It's time for a change
Melodies from Heaven
Rain down on me

When you know better
You do better…

Be like a tree planted by the water
That won't be moved

Go ahead: Rest in Jesus name!

I Started This Journey by Faith

I started this journey by faith as a child
In my mother's womb
I leaped when God called my name

Yes, my name...

Yes, He knew me even then,
The very hairs on my head
He knew and numbered

When I was born the journey of faith continued stronger
In my walk as I learned to listen to His voice
Walk in His way, and I served Him with gladness

Spoke in my Heavenly prayer language of love
To only Him

Only Him...

His spirit filled me with joy, unspeakable joy,
And my faith in Him satisfies my soul

Now and forever more

Selah...

Broken

Emotional abuse, physical abuse, manipulation and control
Are all evil devices used to hurt us and others

To break us down, beat us down
Until we are destroyed and submissive
Making us feel less than human
Broken into a million billion pieces

A broken heart cannot beat strong
Or be in harmonious rhythm
Because being broken and detached
From its core chamber makes you feel
Like crap and worthless

Helpless...

Like scum of the earth

Dirt of the ground and undeserving of love,
Joy, and happiness

The devil is a lie and the father of lies

God says, you are the head and not the tail
Always on top and never beneath
We are fearfully and wonderfully made
Our gifts will make room for us

Trust God...

Only God...

Not man...

The devil comes to kill, steal, and destroy
God comes to give us life and life more abundantly!

Whose Report Will You Believe?

God's love is unconditional and all powerful
Trust and never doubt that God will bring you out

Just over the horizon is a beautiful purple rainbow
With your name on it, so come out of the darkness
Into the marvelous light

No more hiding, trust God's truth
You are; we are somebody in Christ...

God's got our backs and our fronts, He has our hearts
Minds, and souls

That's a beautiful thang, yes that's a peace thang!

God's Spiritual Net

Won't you cast your spiritual net
Out far and wide
Allow God to fill it
With more of His strength…

More of His wisdom…
More of His love, grace, and mercy…
More of His favor…
More of His forgiveness…

God is a great fisher of men
Trust Him to fill your nets and hearts
With more of His Spirit today
Tomorrow and forever more!

God's spiritual net is an ark of safety,
Protection, and provision

Selah…

My God is Faithful

My God is faithful
My God is loving
My God is transparent

My God is real and authentic
My God is perfect in my weakness
My God just is…

It Must Be a God Somewhere

It must be a God somewhere
In order to get through, you have to go through some things
God's word says that after you have suffered a while
God will

Establish you...
Strengthen you...
And settle you...

Know that whatever you are going through
Give God praise in the midst of the storm
Because He cares about bringing you out
Of your situation

Our God is awesome that way!

He can move mountains on our behalf
Show up and show out in all our circumstances

God is a deliverer

God has not forgot aboutcha!

God is still good and worthy to be praised
God is good, and all the time God is good!

He will give you beauty for your ashes...
Give you dancing for your mourning...
Be strength in your weakness...

Peace for your sadness...
Joy for your sorrow...
Be a light house in your darkness
Be your provider in time of plenty and in want

Just rest in Jesus because you know there is a God somewhere!

We Are Blessed Women of God

We are God's Ms. Good Thing and are highly favored by God,
We are strong, mighty, and yet sensitive so be careful
How you do us!

We are wise and have become better not bitter
Due to life's struggles of woman-hood

We have stood tall in the face of adversity and were victorious
We are fearfully and wonderfully made

God may have blessed the man to be the head
Of our households but, He surely broke the mold when
He created woman to be the true hearts of our homes

God does not want us to be beat up physically,
Nor beat down emotionally
God has set us apart because we are predestined
For Greatness in Him

We don't have to prostitute ourselves for drugs,
Money, or what we think may be love

Our bodies are temples of the Holy Ghost and
We are to present them as a pleasing and living
Sacrifice unto God

We are rich blessed Women of God
We are what God says we are
What God has for us, is for us!

We are special, awesome, pure, holy, and upright
We are precious in God's sight

We are beautiful
We are to be loved, cherished, and appreciated

We have grace, compassion, and wisdom
We are sweet, kind, gentle souls

We are prayer warriors
Tearing down many strongholds
We know how to get a prayer through to God.

~We are~ Blessed Women~ of God~

Women of God

Women of God
Remember our Survival is not dependent
On the men in our lives
But are enhanced by them

We are to become joined and enhanced because of them
And yes, allowing feelings of completeness

But no one is suppose to define
Or complete you only God!

Because He is the only perfect and complete ONE!

Women Are Like Diamonds in the Ruff

Women are like Diamonds in the Ruff
We may be a little rough around the edges
But a precious Jewel we are....

We are highly faceted with strength, beauty,
And brilliance like the very Jewels
In God's crown

Just waiting your arrival

We are fearfully and wonderfully made
Handpicked special for God's kingdom

No more are we to think we are damaged goods
But we are good and a little damaged

"We are uniquely made"

"We are Priceless"

"We are human, and make mistakes"

"We are just women; imperfect"

God's Diamonds in the ruff....

From Behind the Veil

Behind the veil is a face of mystery,
A mask of Disguise and depression,
A face of sadness, hurt, rejection,
Pain, and loneliness

The question is what does a happy face look like?
I'm not sure anymore, but if I look deep down
In my soul and search God for the answer
He would tell me your happiness and peace
Lies within me and to count it all joy!

Sometimes when I feel joy it's often snatched away
By depression and rejection
How does one get pass all the rejection
And look toward the face of hope?

God says that He knows the plans He has for you
To give us a future filled with hope
And when we cry, He hears us
And when we are sad he feels us
And when we smile, He smiles

Our Father God knows what we are
And how we are
He cares what we care about

He comes with His arms outstretched and says,
Come here my child come rest
On my bosom and trust and have faith
I will see you through all things

I will rock you ever so sweetly and gently
And give you my tranquil peace that surpasses
All understanding and quietly whisper in your right ear
Peace be still.

But I'm Still Here

The devil satan has been walking about in my life
Trying to kill my spirit, steal my joy,
And destroy my reputation

But I'm still here....

The devil satan is evil and angry because I'm a child of the King
And for Christ I live and for Christ I die

But I'm still here....

The devil satan has tried to bring me down
By always taking things from me, keep me struggling
And feeling like I have no hope for tomorrow

But I'm still here....

The devil Satan
Has tried to keep me sick in my body and my mind depressed,
My heart troubled, my dreams, and visions obscured

But I'm still here....

The devil satan tried to take my joy,
My smile, my peace, my faith

But I'm still here....

The devil satan tried to take my job,
My vehicle, my apartment, my life

But I'm still here....

The devil satan tried to keep me afraid and unhappy

But I'm still here....

I have been mistreated by others
Lied on, cheated on, misused, abused, betrayed
Sabotaged, and misunderstood

But I'm still here....

I'm still here, I'm still standing, I'm still blessed, I'm still alive,
I'm still loved by God; I still have God's favor

I am what God says I am, what God has for me, is for me

It ain't over until God says it's over.
The devil satan is a lie, and the father of lies; the truth is not in
him

My God represents light and truth, and He will hold me up
With His right hand, never to let me go
So devil satan I want you to know
God is still here and I am too
So stop all the madness and just leave me alone!

<u>Some of My Little Favorite Things</u>
<u>That Bring Me Happiness</u>

Happiness is like feeling God's favor upon you every day!
Happiness is enjoying
A hot cup of cocoa on a cold winter's day in front of a warm fire

Happiness is being blessed when others tell you that you're loved
Happiness is enjoying a hot bubble bath by candlelight and jazz

Happiness is enjoying your favorite meal
Topped with your favorite dessert

Happiness is exciting
When you have accomplished something great

Happiness is being curled up with a good book
Or watching your favorite movie

Happiness is enjoying the birth of a child and mother hood
Happiness is beautiful when we fall in love with someone

Happiness is wonderful when we can pamper ourselves
Happiness is being able to bless others

Happiness is enjoying the word of God and singing His praises
Happiness is experiencing God's Shekinah Glory
Happiness is God's angels surrounding you
With His love, peace, and provision

Happiness is reading my Bible, and enjoying worship music
Happiness is enjoying my quiet time with the Lord

Happiness is writing my poetry for others enjoyment
Happiness is one of God's perfect gifts!

CONTENTS
Second Segment

A New Thing

Oh Lord, I'm feeling it's time to do a new thing
A big and wonderful, exciting, joyous new thing

I'm expecting new and fresh possibilities to unfold
Lord, you made the sun to shine
You made the beautiful fragrant aroma of a new day dawning

I am able to breathe the fresh new air of tomorrow
And bask in your tranquil peace

Oh Lord, how great you are
Because you provide me with brand new mercies everyday

You are our fresh manna sent from above
For our daily bread

Lord, I am stepping out on faith
Believing my best is yet to come

Because I know your best is not yet come for me
All because you are doing a new thing!

Deposit of Love

Lord God thank you
For your deposit of love in my heart

My heart is now full of joy
Because of your deposit of love, and I'll never withdraw from it

I'll always be hungry and thirsty for your word
Saturate me with your wisdom

Drench me dripping wet in your oil
Of your anointing

Fill my cup Lord, till I thirst no more
Feed me till I want no more

Bless me with your precious spirit
Today and forever more!

God There Is Nothing Too Hard
For You to Do

Lord God, you are my lover of my soul
You are my compass for Direction
You are my hearts joy

You are hope in my darkness of despair
You are life and light to everything
That I hold near and dear to my heart

Lord God, with you all things are possible
The cattle upon a thousand hills belong to you

Lord God, I thank you for being Alpha and Omega
The beginning and the end
You are in complete control of my life
You rise the sun in the morning, and set the stars
In place at night

You are so awesome!
I am beholding to your glory

There is nothing too hard for you to do
That is why I love you with all my heart!

God's Love Runs for Me So Deeply

God's love runs for me so deeply that many oceans
Cannot quench it, or over take it
It's so deep that it seems so surreal
Finding it hard to believe that such an existence and presence
Is so powerful, He is the Great I AM

God's love runs so deeply it's like a never ending waterfall
That's over flowing continuously
Lord fill my cup till it overflows
In abundance of thee, as the deer pants after the water brook
Let me thirst no more

God's love runs so deeply
That He cares about what we care about
Our inner soul's voice

I feel sometimes like
I have a million-dollar blessing everyday
Receiving God's great unmerited favor and blessings for life

A life in and of God for all eternity
Being financially set for life is having the peace of God
With all your desires and that is priceless

To know you can have everything your heart desires is sheer bliss
And all the happiness your heart and hands can hold
All blessings truly belong to Him above

Blessings of love on earth is God's beautiful masterpiece
That He designed and created giving Him a patent
Forever on our hearts

A debt free life in Jesus is perfection
The calm after the storm is your soul's quietness
From deep within

God's love runs so deep that my adrenaline
In my veins is pumping raging power
It's called God's link and power source

Lord, your love for me is so deep that I shake
My head in marvel, and splendor

My heart is so full that your peace prevails
And fills the atmosphere with praise, peace, and contentment
And then You softly whisper in my ear
Peace be Still...

My Isaac and Ishmael Situation

Lord please make me a Isaac
In the midst of my Ishmael situation

Though my situation is messy at hand, please help me to wait
On your fulfilled promise to work everything out
For my good according to your purpose and plan

Father I know there is nothing to hard for you to do!

Lord God, I thank you for reminding me that I am your Isaac
The "promised one"

Thank you Lord for not forgetting me even when time
Seems to stand still and my patience
Has grown dark and weary

Lord, may your love through your word guide me in hope
As you prepare my destiny

My journey of obedience transforms my past toward my future
Your omnipotent power has manifested your promise
Into the covenant reality of my soul
Despite my short comings

Father, you chose to yet still use me through my trials
For your divine purpose and plan

My true blessing is in the wait, when I surrender my worries
To you for your tranquil peace

Father, I know my timing is not yours and wait I must
To receive your perfect timing
For unto you there is a season for everything

Oh ye child of little faith, trust and never doubt
God surely will bring thee out

Into heights thou has not known;
It's called a new hope of faith....

Behold I am your miracle child of Sara
The mother of all nations!

A Beautiful Fragrant Candle

A beautiful fragrant candle is meant to be lit
Not hidden in a box or covered up, not put in a secret place
Not put under a bed nor a bushel
A candle possesses light in a dark place
Candles light up a dark world

Light is a representation of God in others darkness
A light house is open it can be seen from many miles away
Exuberating illumination for all to see

A beacon of light is the calm after the storm
A candle is to be set on a candle stick to shine and to be seen

A beautiful candle is a fragrant aroma
That brings joy to our sense of smell and our souls

Smile in tranquil peace
Where there is light, there is revelation; God surely is in the midst

Always remember
Some of God's sweet and special treasures to behold
Flowers need to bloom... Birds have to fly...
Diamonds have to sparkle...
Friends provide a soft place to fall...
Candles must be lit to be seen...

I am a lighted candle and a ambassador of the Lord
Bringing you a message of light and hope

May we all be used as God's little candles
To bring forth light, and hope to others all over the world
For continued joy and peace now and forever more.

A God Thang

I am looking forward to becoming better not bitter
Anymore from my life's disappointments
My rejections, my hurts, my pains,
My sadness, and my loneliness

All these things are bitter and negative energy
Piercing my very soul

By thinking and feeling better is positive energy
Gently moving my soul into tranquil peace

For harmonious rhythm and that's a God Thang

Yeah a God Thang!

<u>God Says "My Child of Little Faith"</u>

When I am depressed I have no joy,
No peace, No energy, No strength

I just cry tears of pain that fills a desert that is dry no more
Then God says, "My child wait"

Wait on my lily in the valley to spring forth
It shall over turn your dryness
To a well of living water as only I can give

I'll bottle up every one of your tears
I'll pay it with my own life

So my child of little faith
Be encouraged

Because I am nearer than you think...

God's Direction

Lord, I know I can't let anyone define or determine my destiny
Only YOU!

I want to become impregnated with your design for my life
So that the birth of your desire for my life is manifested

My prayer is to bring the freshness of your word
Into the light for others darkness.

My Shekinah Glory

Let my Shekinah Glory fill you
With more of my sweet tranquil peace
As you rest on the peaceful shores of my love

Listen to my sweet song of praise and say

JESUS is sweet I know!

Heart Print

You have left a heart print upon my life
My heart, Mind, and soul is now forever changed
Because of You!

I am no longer the same, but changed...
Freshly changed and feeling anew with a whisper of calmness
Feeling like a new transformed woman with a hint of hope

My hope is contagious and spreading rapid
To everyone who sees my infectious smile and joy upon my face

All because you have left a heart print upon my life
I'll never be the same and that's a good thing!

What an aha moment, that's a peace thing!

I'm Praying for You

I'm praying for you even when I'm unable to pray for me
By praying for you, allows me to be and feel selfless

When I pray for you it gives me strength to pray for me and others
By praying for you, God sees His love manifested

My prayer for you is: Good health, prosperity, and that God keeps
You in His loving care today, tomorrow, and forever more!

Be Blessed

Loneliness

Loneliness is not just a word or a state of mind it's really real!

Feelings of sadness and depression is sometimes really overwhelming, but God is in the midst

Feelings of joy brings forth happiness and excites the windows Of our souls

We may get lonely but we are never alone with God Right by our sides, reminding us daily that He will Never leave us nor forsake us

God's word says, He knows what we need long before we ask

All we have to do is admit to God that we need help and he acts

Faith is the substance of all things hoped for and the evidence Of things not seen...

Lord I Want

Lord I want to laugh... I want to love... I want happiness...
I want some joy... I want to prosper

I want to be successful... I want to not struggle anymore...
I don't want to hurt anymore...

I want stable job security, no more financial hardship

I want peace of mind

I want to smile again, and make others smile

Lord, I know I want a lot...

But I also know there is nothing too hard for you to do!

So I'll be waiting on my blessings, because receiving your
blessings I know is in the wait

Your word says, Wait, wait on the Lord...

What Will Become of My Life

Lord, what will become of my life?
Will I love another, will I be happy?

Will my love find me? Will we laugh and cry together
Will I have joy?

Will I continue to bring comfort to others?
Will I also be comforted

Will I travel and see the beautiful world
As I collect beautiful things

Will I smile in awe of what may seem like perfection

Lord, please tell me, what will become of my life?

CONTENTS
Third Segment

Prayer Is

Prayer is inviting God to intervene on our behalf
To spend quiet time and talk to God first about everything we face

Take God on all your prayer journey's and allow him
To show up and show out in your life
Our prayers to God are meant to be answered

So stand still and know that God is in control
He is working out everything for our good
According to His riches in glory
So come prayed up and expect a miracle!

Remember we have not because we have asked not….
God is just waiting on us to ask!

You Make My Eyes and Heart Smile

You are the calm in my storm

You are heaven on earth to me
Oh what a joy you are to behold

I am truly blessed because of you
You are my compass for direction

I love you from the depths of my soul

My heart is happy because of you
Despite what my physical eyes may see

You are in complete control of my life and you know
The beginning through the ending of my life's journey

You are…You are…My God!

Your Love Is the Music to My Heart

Your Love is the music to my heart
It provides me with a soft place to fall
My soul finds peace there, oh what joy you bring
You are melodic tranquil waters; I can rest on your peaceful shores

Your sweetness brings forth happiness to my heart and soul
I embellish in awe of your presence oh my how I love thee

When I think of your love for me
I cry tears of joy and my heart is so full
That many oceans cannot quench the thirst I feel
Because of your Love

My heart, mind and soul is yours now and forever more
Thank you for being my safe anchor and harbor
In the midst of trouble storms throughout my life

Thank you Lord for being my power source
When my energy had failed me so many times
You picked me up and dusted me off
You breathed a fresh breath of air into my lungs
Just to remind me that I am still alive and that
I will always be your child.

~Your love is and will always be the music to my heart~

A Wing Injured Bird

I was like a wing injured bird who is hurt and incapacitated
Due to a malfunction of its body part

I am in need of a doctor, a veterinarian to fix and repair
Me to my fullest potential, so I can fly again
My doctor is my father God

Now that I am whole once again I'm able to soar above
The heavens

Lord I am truly strongest when I'm on your shoulders
You help make me more than I thought I could be

You help me to be a better person, you are my hero
My soft place to fall, when I am unable to fly

I must fly now, I must…

Jesus, soar with me in the heavenlies
Fly my little bird fly….

Complete but Not Yet Finished

I'm complete in Jesus; He is the rock of my salvation
In whom I trust and obey
I'm not what I use to be
I'm a new creature
I'm what God says I am

What God has for me, is for me
God has a plan for my life
To give me a future filled with hope

As long as there is breath in my body there is hope
My God is all powerful and complete all by Himself

I am no longer confused
No longer damaged goods, but good and damaged
No longer forgotten, because my Father knows my name

I am whole and complete in Jesus and thank God
He is not done with me yet

He still wants to use me as a vessel to help others
He still wants me to continue on this journey called life

God is my compass for my direction
I have to take one day and one step at a time

My God is truly the Author and Finisher of my faith

I am loved…I am challenged…I am complete in Him…
I am not finished…I am still a work in God's progress of things.

Enemies

The Lord says He will grant the enemies who rise up against you
To be defeated before you, they will come from one direction but
Will flee from you in seven ways

A gentle answer turns away wrath, but a harsh word stirs up anger
Therefore, do not let the sun go down while you are still angry
Because tomorrow is not promised

When a man's ways are pleasing to the Lord
He makes even his enemies live at peace with him
God says gossip separates close friends
With their lies and go down to a man's inner most parts

God will bring justice for his chosen ones
Who cry out to Him day and night
God will not put them off

God says do not do anything that endangers your neighbor's life
For I am the Lord God and I will repay

A heart of peace gives life to the body
Envy rots the bones…

Gods Seed

We are only as good as the seed that the Lord has placed within us
With any seed it takes water to help nourish and cultivate
So it can grow nice and strong to its fullest potential

May we all be like God's little seeds and grow strong
To bring Glory to Him so that the harvest will be
Plentiful and useful to thy hands

Lord, please rain on our fields and produce the harvest
For our good

Oh taste and see that the Lord is good!

He Is the Great I Am

I wish for hope and peace, thy hope is a prayer away
My peace is within You Lord God

Thy joy is sufficient
I wake up each morning because of you Lord God

Lord You supply all my needs
Lord God you are so awesome
Lord You are the Great I am…

Lord I Need

Lord I need your peace that surpasses all understanding
So thy happiness is manifested and I can live my best life

Lord I need to really live, not just exist in a fog of confusion
Please clear up the dark skies, bring forth the sun light
To warm my heart for a better tomorrow in You…

Lord When I'm Alone With You

Lord when I'm alone with you my soul learns worship
Lord when I'm alone with you my soul is in tranquil peace

Lord when I'm with you in my secret place
It is there where I experience your Shekinah Glory, it's so surreal!

When I'm with you joy fills my heart
Many oceans cannot quench the hunger and thirst
I have for You

Lord when I'm alone with you
I speak in my heavenly prayer language just for You
And that makes me feel closer to You
Satan is not welcome, He can't understand
Our sweet beautiful love language
Because it's where only You and I dwell…

Lord You Knew

Lord God, You knew me in my mother's womb
You said, the very hairs on my head are numbered
You know every single strand

You knew I would love You and serve You
You knew I would live for You
You knew I would strive daily
To make you smile like Noah

You knew I would sing your praises
You knew I would rest my head on your bosom
When I would start to feel scared

You knew my gifts would make room for me
You knew the only true peace I would have
Would be in You!

~Lord You just knew~

Open My Eyes Lord

Open my eyes Lord that I may see
Open my ears Lord that I may hear
Open my heart Lord that I may heal
Open my soul to absorb your word
Open my mind to receive your wisdom

Open ye gates that I may dwell in your presence
Lord, please soften my heart from bitterness
So I can become better and not bitter

Lord deliver me from fear
Lord just please love me unconditionally!

Trouble Won't Last Always

Trouble won't last always
Because God is not the author of confusion

Trouble won't last always
Because God is ordering my steps

Trouble won't last always
Because God lives and I can face tomorrow

Trouble won't last always
Because no weapon formed against me shall prosper

Trouble won't last always
Because God is my strength and refuge
An ever present help in the time of trouble

Trouble won't last always
Because I ask God to look beyond all my faults and see my needs

Trouble won't last always
Because God says He knows the plans He has for us
To give us a future filled with hope

Trouble won't last always
Because God knows my name and it is written
In the lamb's book of life

Trouble won't last always
Because God has given His angles charge over my life
For safety and protection

Trouble won't last always
Because He makes even our enemies live at peace with us

Trouble won't last always
Because truthful lips endure forever

But a lying tongue only last for a moment

Trouble won't last always
Because we walk by faith and not by sight

Trouble won't last always
Because those who try to kill the body
Cannot kill the soul of God's children

Trouble won't last always
Because when we are in God and lay down at night
Our sleep will be sweet

Trouble won't last always
Because when we pass through the waters
It won't over take us, when we walk through the fire
We will not be burned

Trouble won't last always
Because our heavenly Father knows what we need
Long before we ask

Trouble won't last always
Because the righteous cry out and the Lord hears them
He delivers them from all their troubles

Trouble won't last always
Because the Lord will make you the head and not the tail
Blessing you to be at the top and never at the bottom

Trouble won't last always,
Because you will be blessed going out and coming in

Trouble won't last always
Because thy word is a lamp
To my feet and a light for my path

Trouble won't last always,
Because when we delight ourselves in the Lord

He will give us the desires of our heart

Trouble won't last always
Because whether we turn to the right or to the left
Your ears will hear a voice behind you saying
"This is the way my child, walk in it"

Trouble won't last always,
Because when we give, it will be given back to us
In good measure, pressed down, shaken together
And running over

Trouble can't last always,
Because God is too powerful to allow trouble for eternity

He wants His Glory to be seen and manifested
He who believes in Him will have everlasting life!

A Prayer of Hope

Lord I'm ready to start a fresh new beginning
I'm anxious to be happier

To feel appreciated and to have a peace of mind
I desire to know what I am to do
And how to make new plans for my life

To smile, to laugh again, to feel hopeful about tomorrow
To gain new perspectives about my life

To have goals to reach them
To dare to dream
To say that I have a dream

Desiring joy and unspeakable joy deep down in my soul
So I can truly live and not just exist…

Embrace Your Struggle

Lord break me so you can make me
Make me so you can mold me
Mold me so I'm obedient to you and your word

Let the struggle of my life
Teach me some perspectives and Godly wisdom
So I can truly value myself through the hurt and pain
Life has thrown at me

I am who God says I am
I am not bitter but better

I'm broken and damaged but I'm still a good person
You continue to tell me that I'm good and valued by You

I'm embracing my struggles
Because it is there I find my real strength, and worth
Lord thank you for my struggles because
It's there where I found You!

I met and found Jesus through the most difficult times
Of my life, the areas where I have had the most pain.

Lord thank you for the struggles
So I could truly embrace a saved and Christian life.

~To God be the glory for the things He has done~

CONTENTS
Fourth Segment

Father in Your Presence

Father in your presence
I am beholding your glory upon my face as Moses
Loving and adoring you

Oh Lord, there is none like You
Longing for your sweet peace
On the tranquil shores of your love

I lay aside and surrender every weight
So you can carry me in your arms
To Glory land where I bask in the meadows
Of beautiful orchids and violets
While experiencing your pure serene happiness

My heart finds peace there so I can rest
I feel as if I am wrapped in a blanket of your love

In my meditation today, I stand in awe of You
Because I know I'm protected by You
I smile and exhale with joy and splendor
At the thought of your precious Heavenly presence

Father, You are truly the King above all names
There is none like You,
I sincerely thank You from the depths of my heart
For being the one, true lover of my soul…

God's People Are All Just Human

Lord, we make so many mistakes
We fail daily, we sin daily, and we all have issues
But, with God all things are possible

We can have hope in the midst of the storms in this life
Lord I take comfort in your strength

It is there we learn peace and contentment
That helps develop us spiritually
To see your plan and provision for our lives
As You fill us with your love and bless us
With your joy, grace, and mercy

Lord You are a real God, for my real problems
For a real future

After all we are just human not perfect
We have yet not arrived just imperfect
We are your creation belonging to You...

I Am What God Says I am

I am blessed...I am teachable...I am worthy...

I am the head and not the tail, always on top
Never on the bottom

I have character, integrity, and wisdom
I am God's creation and master piece

I am fearfully and wonderfully made
I am special and unique

I am strong because God gives me strength
I am God's heart and He is mine

I pray to Him and He hears me
I am not perfect; I am still His just as I am...

Lord God, I'm so Glad You Called My Name

Lord because I am not just a hearer,
I am a doer of your voice and word

I am blessed because you called my name…my name…

I can rest better now because you whispered in my ear
Peace be still…

Father I'm so glad you knew me in my mother's womb

I leaped for joy when You called my name…my name…

My Daily Prayer

This is the day that the Lord hath made
I will rejoice and be glad in it
This is His day and I will rejoice

May the God of Abraham, Isaac, and Jacob smile
Upon me and others today, tomorrow, and forever more

Lord the cattle on a thousand hills belong to You
Please bless me with your unmerited favor

Look beyond all my faults and see my needs

Please send your fresh manna from Heaven
So that I may learn to trust You and only You.

Some of God's Amazing Miracles

A new day dawning brings fresh air for our tomorrows
The new birth of a baby is precious
Just as your miracle Son "Jesus"

The ocean is wide and deep, just like your love for us
Living this life saved and serving you is amazing
Because you are so amazing to me

To experience your wonderful blessings from above
Is special and incredible

Where would I be without you?
I never want to find out

I never want to be out of your will
I never want to experience being from your grace

Lord I always want to experience more of you and your miracles.

Sing Me Melodies from Heaven

Sing me a new song of hope and peace
Sing me praises of love and joy

Sing me beautiful rivers and streams
That bring me tranquil quiet moments
To make me smile

Let the rhythm of the rain make sweet music
Upon my heart

Sing me melodies from Heaven that lifts my hands
To worship You.

Springs Is In the Air

A beautiful warm quiet sunny day is God's whisper of love
He has bestowed upon us this day

He has given us a hint of hope with a sprinkle of peace
Just to remind us that He is always there

Indeed, spring is in the air....

The tomorrow's of our future is tucked away in God's bosom
Just awaiting the entrance to our eye gates...ear gates...
Even our heart gate of our inner soul's voice

Enjoy, welcome, and embrace God's beautiful creation
Of a new day dawning

Indeed, spring is in the air...

The Pain of My Heart

Dear Lord, please take the pain of my heart
Carry it in your hands today, for I'm at your mercy

Please look beyond all my faults and see my needs
I ask favor, honor, and validation of others

I know I have your love and respect and I know who's I am

Father my prayer today is to let my light so shine
Before You and others that You may see my good works

Father take all my fears away and cast them in the bottom
Of the sea of forgetfulness to be remembered no more

I just ask that you rain on my field of despair and release
The need that my harvest maybe useful and plentiful
To thy hands

Lord, thank you for hearing my cry for help
I know and trust that my help is on the way
Because the pain of my heart needs a release for peace
That only You can give

Thank you Lord for your love today
My heart is now full of gladness because of You

To God be the Glory for the things He has done!

The Captain of the Ship Is Jesus

The captain of the ship is Jesus
As long as He is on board you have nothing to worry about
He even commands the winds, waves, and the seas to obey

He rebukes the weather
When the waters are troubled
He says,
"Peace be still"
Then a sudden calm comes over the storm
Causing things to come subject to Him

How mighty are you Lord...
How precious are you Lord...
How worthy are you Lord...

Jesus with you keeping watch over me
I worry about nothing
All my troubles are over

There is a peace that comes over me
As only you can provide
Peace be still you say

Tranquil smooth waters abound
My is life calmer
Soothing moments abide

Healing comes to me
Joy spreads through my veins
All because
You are the captain of my ship...

<u>*I Desire God's Hands Upon My Life For...*</u>

I desire God's hands upon my life
Through His Spirit of protection

For repentance and forgiveness
For my very existence and salvation

For His safety and provision
For light in my darkness
For guidance and direction
For joy, grace, and mercy

For love and peace
For my blessings
For my dreams and prophecies

For vision and creativity
For praise and worship
For my sweet rest

For sweet communion
For hope and truth
For knowledge and wisdom

For relationship with Him
For my good health and strength
For understanding

For prosperity and favor to bless others
For motivation and inspiration

I just desire God's hands upon my life
Forever and ever....

God Has

God has a patent on our hearts and lives
When we trust and belong to Him

As the deer pants for the water brook
We too pant for God's love and favor

God has blessed our going out
He has blessed our coming in

God has given me a Heavenly prayer language
Just for our sweet communion
No one else is there but me and Him in the throne room
It's called our secret place

God has so richly blessed me with my very life
To serve Him

God has looked beyond my faults and He sees my needs
God has never failed me yet

I dare you to try Him for yourself!

Always Remember

Always remember that God has a plan A, B, and C
Always remember that God is not finished with us yet
We are still His work in progress here on earth

Always remember that God is our power source
To overcome our problems
Always remember that God is just a prayer away

Always remember God made us to be the head and not the tail
To be on top, and never on the bottom

Always remember God came to give us life
And life more abundantly
Always remember with God all things are possible

Always remember God knows the plans He has for us
To give us a future and a hope

Always remember to thank God for our daily bread
Always remember to thank God daily
For our very life, health and strength

Just always remember
That God is....

God's Agape Love

God's agape love is an unselfish love
It expects nothing in return
God's love is unconditional toward us
He proved His love when He went to the cross for our sins

It's the gift that keeps on giving
It's not man made its God made
It's more than the love we express to others
When we show love on Valentine's Day
Or the love that the Chinese express on
Chinese New Year called Hong-Bao
When they give red packets or money
To their loved ones

God's agape love is much more powerful, it's sacred
It's holy, it's omnipotent
It's priceless, it's peaceful
It's precious, it's miraculous
It's perfection, it's melodic and tranquil
It's unspeakable joy; it's a covenant with us
It's pure and honest; it's an eternal life with Him
It's showing real love from Him to us
It's His light to a dark world
It's His real power, for our real problems
It's the significant source that can only be linked
When we become linked with Him
It's being blessed and highly favored
True Agape Love

God's word says,
If we love one another all men will know
We are His disciples.

To Expect a Miracle

Expect God to show up and show out
In all your circumstances of life

Expect the imaginable, expect the miraculous
Expect the element of surprise
Expect faith and action

Expect God's favor, expect blessings,
Expect joy, unspeakable joy
Expect God not to close a door
Without opening a new window of hope

Expect brand new mercies each and everyday
Expect the peace that surpasses all understanding

Expect that when you knock at God's door
That He will answer

Go to God and expect results!

CONTENTS
Fifth Segment

Down In the Well of Depression

Down in the well of depression
Is dark and cold
Is scary and desolate
Is without hope
Is full of pain
Is without no signs of life
Is dry and leaves you thirsting for water
Is my tears way out toward the healing of my soul…

God's Adrenaline in My Veins

God's adrenaline in my veins is powerful…
Is hopeful…
Is peaceful…
Is eternal…

Is joy, unspeakable joy…
Is strong…
Is faithful…

Is rhythm-matic…
Is harmonious…
Is precious…

Is sweet…
Is loving…
Is tranquil…

Is priceless…
Is trusting…
Is forgiving…

Is all I will ever want and need…

My Moses Burning Bush Experience

My Moses burning bush experience came one night
When I didn't know how I was going to make it
I saw no light at the end of the dark tunnel of my life
I was depressed, scared and lonely,
I was without a job to make ends meet

Almost homeless…
I felt worthless…
I thought I was on the brink of self-destruction

When God stepped in and said,
My child you are standing on my Holy ground
And you will not be burned alive…

You may go through some things, but in order to get through
You have to go through…
These things you are experiencing will not over take you
Nor will you be consumed with fire
You will live and not die…

Did I not send you fresh manna from Heaven
When you were hungry…

Trust and know that I will bring you out
Over and through this struggle as only I can do
Trust and never doubt my love for you is eternal…

Your blessing is on the way
I say wait, wait on the Lord and be of good courage…

"This is only a test!"
A test of your faith…

Faith is the substance of all things hoped for and the evidence
Of things not seen…
I am here…I am here…

Only God

Throughout some very hard times in my life
I had to do things by myself
Thank God I was never alone because my Father God
Was with me the whole entire time

He promised to never leave me, nor forsake me

He was my anchor and my strength
Holding me up with his hands
Every step of the way

I could not have gone through hard and difficult times
Any other way

So I say,
Thank God…
Praise God…
And only God…

Loving Me So Unconditionally

Lord, I had another sleepless night feeling hurt, rejected,
Disappointed, sad, depressed, and abandoned
No one really knows my pain or my heart issues
Well at least that's how I feel sometimes

I know in my heart of hearts you know God!
You know God…

You really know my aching heart
Thank you Lord for loving me so unconditionally
Even when others don't or at least I think they don't love me.

When Lord, When?

I don't know if I will ever have love again
Better yet,
If the right one will come to find me

I have always chosen the wrong men and always end up alone
I pray for my real Boaz to find me
To profess his love for me

But he never comes…
That makes my heart sad sometimes

My heart is in so many broken pieces
It's too many to count

When Lord?
When will I experience my true love

My Boaz…
My heart's joy…
My husband…

When Lord, when?
Oh my God in Heaven
When Lord, when?

When the Praise Comes from Deep Down In Your Belly

When the praise comes from deep down in your belly it's powerful
It's a mature praise, not as a child like praise
It's the praise that reaches the debts of your inner soul
Your worship is for real and strong
It gives you the ugly cry that you can't hold back

It's the place where God dwells and gets his attention
That you mean business and God reacts accordingly
It shows true sincerity of your heart

It expresses repentance
It shows God that you are serious
About new life changes you need to make
To become broken so God can really use you

Down in your belly is where true worship and adoration
Reigns supreme
God stands up and takes notice
That you need more of his spirit and strength

Praise out of your belly is the greatest praise ever
It's so amazing and melodic
Praise out of your belly to our mouth into God's ears
He listens attentively

It's deeply felt and ushers in healing and deliverance
Praise out of your belly
Is God's way of cleansing you from the inside out

In order to clean a fish, you must first catch it
That is how God cleans us
He catches us and purges us so that we become subject to Him
For direction as only He can do!

It's Really Gotten Old

Lord things have really gotten old
I'm sick and tired and tired and sick
Of the same old stuff just on a different day
Please do a new thing in my life!

What a rollercoaster ride
That is going on in my mind
Lord God you are not the author of confusion
So please take over and smooth the troubled waters

My mind needs peace…

Sometimes I feel like there is no win-win…
But to settle is not what I want to do
Please help me to be more patient

Wait I must; you say,

I so desire to get things right in my life finally
Because things have really gotten old!

Out with the old and in with the new
That's what I need
A new thing, a God Thang
Yep a God thang!!

Lord Just A Glimpse A Peak

Lord if you could give me just a glimpse
A peak of what my life will be like

What would I see?

Would I see hope?

Would I see Love?

Would I see happiness?

Would I see joy?

Would I see You?

I just pray for a glimpse, a peak of your spirit shinning
Like a beacon light as a light house
Bidding me to come closer so I can experience such a deep
Warmth in my heart

More of You;

I have a song in my heart that stands the test of time,
It transcends time
How I long for sweet melodies from you that never ends

My hope is in you and I look forward to seeing a glimpse
A peak of Your Spirit

Can I come and touch the hem of Your garment
So I can be made whole

Oh yes Lord, thy peace is sufficient.

Another Day of Hope

Lord, I awakened to another day in You
Another day that I feel hopeful
Another day for some awesome news
Some good news
I just want another day
That I could feel appreciated and valued

I want to live, just not exist…
Yes, another day of hope

Hope for another day
What will tomorrow bring?

Well, just another day in you, alive and well
Is more than enough

You have already done more than enough
Thy grace is sufficient!

You're Never Alone

Close your eyes and imagine that our Father God
Was walking along side of you on a sandy white beach

Holding your right hand telling you that you can make it
That you can do all things through Christ that strengthens you

Imagine basking on God's peaceful shores of his shoulders
Regaining more strength than you ever thought was possible

Just imagine His still small voice whispering to you
I love you my child, I love you more today,
Than yesterday, but not as much as tomorrow

Imagine your tears became His tears and filled your heart
With tranquil peace and providing you with a soft place
To fall because He cares for you

He promised to never leave you nor forsake you
Making you sweet promises like
I'll make you the head and not the tail
Reassuring you that you'll always be on the top
And never on the bottom

All because He never wants you to feel alone

When you start to feel the daily pressures of life just remember
To close your eyes for a moment, reflect that you're never alone

You're never alone!
Because our Father God is with you
Now and forever more
Selah…

God Thank You for Your Love

Lord God please hold me in your arms
Can I soak in your loving strong arms?

You are the love of my life
And…
The life of my love
Thank you God for your love

Thank You!

Lord I Like My Quiet Time With You

It's tranquil…
It's peaceful…
It's beautiful…

It's my solitude; it allows me to think quietly
With no noise
I bask in pure delight
It's comfortable

I'm relaxed
It's as if I'm in a meadow full of beautiful flowers
Taking in the joy they bring
Quietness rejuvenates me because I can think
On God's word and promises for my life

There is nothing more satisfying than feeling peaceful
Deep down in my soul

My heart smiles of happiness
My eyes twinkle with excitement
My mind is renewed

My quiet time is God's way of saying
Thank you for spending some quality time with me today
God longs for sweet intimacy with me
Just me and Him

He talks with me and tells me that I am His own
He reminds me of His love for me
And I remind Him of my love for Him

It's a wonderful and beautiful thing
What God and I have together is "special"
I rest on His peaceful shores
Because it's the place where God dwells and reigns supreme.

Thank you Lord for my quiet time in You
I don't like to be too busy that I can't make time for You
Lord, my quietness is my way to find You
I awe and exhale because I know
You have my back

Thank you my dear Lord
For making my quiet times so special

To God be the Glory for the things He has done
And not yet done!

Loudly Misunderstood

I say Ta'mato, you say To'mato
Apples are not oranges,
Oranges are not apples
Words are words
Until you give them a voice
Of definition to be heard

Saying what you mean and meaning what you say
Well it's just leaves no error for misunderstanding

When a person is specific and direct
Causes the brain to process the information
For what it is and leaving no error
For confusion, complications, or difficulty

Being understood quietly makes for loud interpretation
That makes my heart glad and my mind satisfied
My eyes smile when you get what I'm saying
Therefore, I become peaceful when you loudly understand me

So instead of talking loud and saying nothing
Try talking loud and saying everything
That makes sense from me to you from my intellect to yours
Being understood causes tranquility and the meeting of the minds
Receives joy because you get me, and I get you!

God's word says life and death is in the power of the tongue
So it's wise to use wisdom when we talk to one another,
Our words to others can speak life to us or tear us down

Expressing encouragement builds us up, belittling tear us down
Compliments are meant to make us smile
Smiling is good medicine for our souls,
So let's all try to loudly understand
With quiet ears and hearts
So that we really understand the right way.

I am truly strongest
When I'm on your shoulders and You raise me up!

I long for the day
When I'm correctly and properly understood
That will be a perfect day…

It's kinda like experiencing butter on toast…
Fresh coffee in the morning…
Peaches in a peach cobbler…
Ice cream and cake…
Cornbread with my greens…

Your ying to my yang,
You now get my drift
It's called perfection!

I May Cry, but I Won't Die...

I may cry but I won't die
From the lack of your love
The lack of your touch
The lack of your embrace
The lack of your support and understanding
The lack of your words saying
I'm proud of you and you done good, real good
The lack of your smile in your eyes
When you think of my accomplishments

I may cry but I won't die
I had to give birth to this vision
Because I've been pregnant for so long
For over forty years with this word hidden
In my soul and in my belly
Blessed living waters reside there

It was time, my time to birth this baby
Of Poetry to the world
Because God knew it was good...
Real good!

God said it was necessary for my good
Necessary for my healing of hurt, pain, and rejection of you

My blood, sweat, and tears of laboring this word was needed
To bring me to where I was suppose to be
Which is right here
Right here with God by my side
Holding my hand through it all...

Everything that I had to go through
Was for His purpose of recognition right now

Right here no matter who was not with me
On this journey of self-awareness and hope

God's word says that His grace is sufficient for you!
So you see your lack of love and embrace
Brought me closer to God's arms
Of protection, strength
And His unconditional love

God gave me more strength than I ever knew I had
More peace that surpasses my own understanding
God desired more of me and more of me He got
Because of your lack of love and embrace

I may cry, but I won't die
Because I choose to live and survive
Without the love and support of others
Who claim they love me
When it suits them…

Praise God that He has unconditional love for me
Because your love comes with conditions
That God isn't apart of!

I need and require more unconditional love
No matter what I may have said and done
In my past of mistakes
Charge it to my head and not my heart
Because I need your love
Your unconditional love…

Love me because you should!
God expects and requires that we love
The greatest of the commandments
Is to love one another
Despite our faults and shortcomings

Just love me because you should, unconditionally!

Well, God knows I'm not perfect and have flaws
Yet, I have a big loving heart
That God gave me to love you with

No matter how bad you treat me…
So with that being said;
I promise I may cry, but I won't die
Because God isn't finished with me yet!!

Lord Please Bless Me Anyhow

Lord please bless me anyhow
I know I may not deserve it sometimes
But I can sure use it because I need a breakthrough
So I can truly be delivered and healed

I so want to receive your miracles
Oh Lord, bless me indeed
Enlarge my territory,
Keep your hand upon me

Bless my going out and my coming in
And please give me the desires of my heart
I am your child and You are my God

And I promise to serve you
With all my heart, mind, and soul
Today, tomorrow and forever more

Please God
Just bless me anyhow
If you want to
Please want too…

<u>To My Reader</u>

God has impregnated me with the vision of a series of books and now it's time to push and deliver this word out to others!

The manifestation is real and the birth of these books is here! My vision of inspiration by the Holy Spirit and through God is now tangible in written form.

I pray you all enjoy my blood, sweat, and tears; through the pathway of my healing journey while you embrace my future wholeness.

God was and is always there for me every step of the way. It's not in my strength, but I am able in His strength.

Less of me and more of Him! Praise God that He is not finished with me yet. There is still hope as long as there is breath in my body, there is hope…

www.ingramcontent.com/pod-product-compliance
Lightning Source LLC
Chambersburg PA
CBHW060359050426
42449CB00009B/1807